WomensWords

THE POWER OF A WOMAN

Edited by

Joanne Baxter

First published in Great Britain in 2000 by
WOMENSWORDS
Remus House, Coltsfoot Drive,
Woodston,
Peterborough, PE2 9JX
Telephone (01733) 898101
Fax (01733) 313524

HB ISBN 0 75430 865 0
SB ISBN 0 75430 866 9

FOREWORD

Although we are a nation of poetry writers we are accused of not reading poetry and not buying poetry books: after many years of listening to the incessant gripes of poetry publishers, I can only assume that the books they publish, in general, are books that most people do not want to read.

Poetry should not be obscure, introverted, and as cryptic as a crossword puzzle: it is the poet's duty to reach out and embrace the world.

The world owes the poet nothing and we should not be expected to dig and delve into a rambling discourse searching for some inner meaning.

The reason we write poetry (and almost all of us do) is because we want to communicate: an ideal; an idea; or a specific feeling. Poetry is as essential in communication, as a letter; a radio; a telephone, and the main criterion for selecting the poems in this anthology is very simple: they communicate.

CONTENTS

RESIGNATION

She stands there, small and shabby,
Grey hair, white face wrinkled
With care and poverty.
She clutches the PVC bag
In which a plastic purse
Contains inadequate pension.
Grey as her hair, the sky
Presses down, chilling thin bones
Ill-protected under threadbare coat.
She peers, with eyes now dulled
From stitching shirts beneath a naked bulb,
Up the empty tarmaced street.

The 'bus which should have come
Ten minutes since, is not in sight.
Sheeting rain stings parchment skin.
Head bowed and shoulders hunched,
Like a small grey mouse
She scuttles home.
At six, watching her black and white TV,
She learns there was a drivers' strike.
Shopping unaccomplished she scans her shelf
Then heats a can of onion soup for tea.

Vivien Bayley

SHELTER

it seems that once I knew true perfection, bliss, ecstasy - I knew flight
and I knew how to live quietly, internally.

let go of whatever longing and sad aching pines your soul
                                                so thin and fine.
let the winds and waves part peacefully for you, disintegration may
begin again and pass through you without harm, purifying to a
simplicity you may never have known, you have forgotten to know.

it must come that you and I will meet again beyond the silent cities,
still resisting the untenable tension of time and force of pace, and
make our way home, in each other's arms. rest with me, now you
know who I am, now you know you can. I can touch the ground
and never know where this earth's end comes and goes, infinity is
freedom, peace and sure stillness what we'll only need, breathing
in sweet, slow harmony; the perfect heart of you inside the sun
of your eye, and my mind made easy by the touch of its simple
glow of radiance.

solitude and times of growth, respite, a momentary pause to
catch ourselves, breathless. grass waves softly, flowers thrive and waste
as it ever was, there's no need for us, young and strong and alive,
to think of how we'll die. let there be nothing in your mind, nothing
except the song of you and I, the new earth of our plain sense,
and the void of blissful, shining quiet.

Mandi Kristjen Tweedy

NOON

(After a painting by Vincent Van Gogh)

Slumber sweetly, dearest maiden
after the long hours of toil.
I am resting here beside you,
and will keep you from all ill

Cattle feeding, cart unladen,
all is quiet this midday break.
Shoes abandoned, sickles dormant.
Back to work when we awake.

Scything, tying, stacking, reaping,
through the seeming endless day.
Long the hours to gather harvest,
'neath the sun's relentless rays.

Hands and faces, scratched and dirty,
bodies bent, from gathering grain.
All must be safely gathered in,
before the coming rain.

Limbs grow tired, eyes near closing.
Will there ever be respite?
Here we labour, hardly pausing,
'til the very close of night.

Worn and weary, trudging homeward,
thankful that the work is done.
Dusk now dims the daytime shadows
and another battle's won.

Pam Dawkins

A USED PURSE

Great Aunt Violet
had this purse
its short chain
once was silver.
She carried
a dance card,
an invite,
and a tiny pencil.

Aunt Sunny
used the purse
for pot, incense,
hair bands, a peace sign,
a beaded necklace.

I found it
in my gram's hat boxes
after she passed into the clouds.
I slip in two condoms,
lipstick, Vaseline,
hairspray, a key,
a mobile phone.

Which daughter will carry
a revolver,
credit cards, pills, wedding rings,
plane tickets
inside it?

Finn Wiitala

1899 To 1999

Women back 100 years,
Did as they were told, had many fears,
Their dresses down around the floor,
Got in the way when doing their chores,
To show an ankle, God forbid,
Were frowned upon the ones who did,
Move on to 1939 the war years started,
No more fun,
Women had to do their bit,
Working in factories, showing true grit,
Now 1960s, flowers in hair,
With freedom of love, mini skirts, legs so bare,
Much music and drugs all going around,
Some sleeping rough on hard, hard ground,
Now come the '90s and life has now changed,
Women have top jobs,
We do have *some* brains,
We find the strength to work and have fun,
To take us into the *new millennium*,
Well, that's a challenge we all hope to bear,
If we all pull together,
We can say, *we'll get there.*

Elsie Kemp

GETTING THERE

An old photograph seemed to catch my eye,
Causing me to reflect
And ponder times gone by.
I thought about how things have changed;
How women have come so far
From feeling 'somewhat walked on'
To having 'quite a bit of power'.
From kitchen worktop to lap-top
From kitchen sink to behind a desk
That's just the beginning - now listen to the rest.
Equality of professions, never heard of before
With salaries slowly catching up, of course we'd still like more!
We have our place in politics - Prime Minister - a she?
We've been to the moon as well - amazed those in the photo would be.
'In their day' who'd have looked after the family
Had there been much choice of work?
With little or no choice of childcare
It's a decision they'd have had to shirk.
The unmarried mum - 'the girl in a mess!'
No longer hidden away - thank God we've progressed.
So let us move on, put that photo at bay,
With hope, as we head for the year 2K.
May we all strive for what is best
And let 2000 be the ultimate test.

Janice Sheppard

MY RECOLLECTIONS OF DAYS GONE BY

Currants and sugar in blue paper bags
No fancy trimmings, no extra tags
Not many sweeties, they were on ration
Clothes to suit but not in fashion
Hard-working parents, my mum and dad
Feeding us well on the little they had
Outside loos were down the yard
Happy times although quite hard
No hot water, the tin bath on the wall
One bathfull washed us all
No televisions and no telephone
Doorsteps scrubbed with donkey stone
Children were smacked when they were naughty
Pennies per pound were two hundred and forty
Folk helped each other in neighbourly ways
They're now long gone with the good old days

Eileen Garnett

WOMAN

How could they be,
So knowing and yet unwise?
Women's fight for freedom,
Had to overcome male pride.

Their unfulfilled dreams,
Ideas they had to hide,
Kept secret inside their minds,
Like a spring, ready to unwind.

Never underestimate the power of womankind,
A 100 years from slave to queen,
She has only just begun,
To live her dream of freedom.

Jane Wilks

TELLING GREAT-GRANDMA

You'll never believe me, Great-Grandma
when I tell what the century brought
to women from all social backgrounds
who have choices which you did not

Of course, you knew about suffragettes,
well, in 1918 we were granted the vote
eventually marching to equal rights
challenging men of every note

Professional women rank at the top
as ministers of country and church
astronauts voyaging heavens and stars
sportswomen, doctors, judges at court

Sex is flaunted in chat and books
and birthing done without pain
babies can grow in little glass tubes
or be prevented by taking a pill

There are noisy machines for daily chores
and we create quality time for play
with our children, who are minded by others
whilst we work in a different way

Women still die from lumps in the breast,
although others can be given new hearts,
some may suffer from symptoms of stress
(a new word for thinking too hard)

There are still one or two situations
for women to resolve, as they can,
before facing the fight of next century,
yes, that's it, 'Equal Rights for Men'

Elizabeth Main

A CENTURY'S PROGRESS

As the twentieth century finally draws to a close
It gives us pause to look back and observe
A hundred years of human history
Women's progress on an upward curve

'Having it all', working to the top or staying at home
The choices are ours to make
Positive role models now abound
It is up to us to ensure which preference we take

We have found our voice with which to proclaim
Our hopes and needs we now express
No longer do we wait in vain
Instead we move forward expecting no less

The new millennium gives us all the chance
To tread our own individual paths to self-fulfilment
A sense of pride in our achievements thus far
For further progress indeed we are meant

Paula Drummond

MY BEST FRIEND

A hundred years ago it's true,
Life was very different for people just like you.
Washing, cleaning, cooking and shopping was the way,
But no labour-saving helpers to get you through the day.

Dolly tubs and possers, mangles and hard soap,
Red, chapped hands with no soft cream to use to help you cope,
And then a line of washing, hanging up so high,
Above the fire, on a rack, hoping it will dry.

What a different life we lead in 1999,
Here I sit with glass in hand, sipping lovely wine,
While my gorgeous automatic is whirling round and round,
Thank you lovely washer, you're worth every flippin' pound!

Dorothy Chodan

WHO'S CONNING WHO?

A new millennium will soon arrive
In it we're told, women will thrive
A better place for them than others
Their battling grans and radical mothers.

Women who fought for rights they now enjoy -
But is it just a clever ploy
To trap them in another way
Doubling the work women do each day?

Once housewives were proud to describe
Their useful working lives inside
But now it's received with a sneer
Thinly disguised as 'domestic engineer'.

Should women perform a daily balancing act?
Men wouldn't do it and that's a fact
Women should be free to choose
And whatever their choice they shouldn't lose.

Nor should they be the victims of discrimination
From members of their own generation
Child-rearing should not be usurped
Nor those who do it over-worked.

All women need recognition
Society benefits from good intuition
A working woman or a stay-at-home mum
Both share a role in the new millennium.

Charmaine Fletcher

RIPPLE

With a dormant mirrored surface,
The lake lies still and cool,

Then at a given moment,
It unravels like a spool,

The hoop-like waves get bigger,
As they glide across the top,

And once its move has started,
It has no power to stop,

With ever widening circles,
The ripples' path will go,

Speeding out across the lake,
Its watery life to show,

And with a fleeting passion,
It makes its gentle dance,

Because it never comes again,
Like us, it has one chance,

Time moves on, and it's no more,
This brief encounter spend,

Just for one lovely moment,
Its beauty it has lent,

A kiss upon the waiting bank,
Will end this magic spell,

It's one of nature's miracles,
That we all know so well.

Duchess Newman

UNTITLED

One hundred years of progress
A millennium of strife
Has brought changes unimaginable
To the quality of feminine life
In AD 1900, the world was a different place,
Women weren't allowed opinions,
They were just a pretty face.
Their days were long and arduous
Home comforts they were rare,
The things we take for granted
Well, they just were not there!
All the electrical gadgets
That now not owning is a sin
Were entirely out of the question -
There was nowhere to plug them in!
In the corner of your kitchen
Where your Bendix proudly stands
There stood a wooden dolly tub
Where you dipped your reddened hands.
You'd scrub your clothes with sunlight soap
On a washboard till they were clean
Now, aren't you glad that you were born
After the invention of the washing machine?
As we approach the year 2001
What inventions will be spanking new?
Perhaps they'll invent a super machine
That will iron and hang clothes up too!

M Finch

THE AGE OF INNOCENCE

When I look at my memories of yesterday,
I remember the harshness of womanhood.
No modern conveniences did we have.
The years spent in the kitchen;
Cooking and cleaning took all day long.
What I would have done
For a microwave, a vacuum cleaner, a washer or dryer.
But such things were as far beyond my imagination
As man landing on the moon.
And as for a career, well it was a man's job
To provide for his family.
And yet, despite the harshness,
Memories of happier times resurface;
Of climbing trees and carving names
Of running through meadows and paddling in streams.
The picking of bluebells and chasing of my dreams.
Despite the opportunities for the women of tomorrow,
A part of me still grieves for the
Lost age of innocence
That womanhood brings.

Caroline E Ashton

RENAISSANCE GIRLS

So you want to belong to that leisured class
who say 'isn't' not 'ain't' and put 'ah' in 'glass';
who in summer decide where to deepen their tan
and who choose the right clothes to attract the right man;
who think about colour of carpet and curtain
and add the right spice when the cookbook's uncertain;
whose run-around cars pick the kids up from school
and who understand teenagers' need to be cool;
who can tell apart Beethoven, Bach and the rest
but on Saturday night can shake arse with the best;
who can throw a good party or host a reception,
are modern in all that concerns contraception;
who keep all their tact yet can still be outspoken;
can work on a men's team yet never be 'token';
can speak after dinner in one foreign language
and manage another to ask for a sandwich;
who used to play saxophone, possibly strings
and who pay that bit extra for STs with 'wings';
who wear make-up for funerals, weddings and clubs
but get out the old jeans to eat luncheons in pubs,
play a good game of pool and will beat you at darts
and could write you a critique of film or fine arts;
who make quite a nice sum from interior design
or the marketing side of the import of wine;
who can horse ride and bike ride; who shower twice a day
and for every occasion have something to say;
it's the Renaissance Girls, 'Cosmopolitan' 's lists -
it's a class of all-rounders that barely exists:
all the covers scream 'this could be you!' so you buy,
just to read on the first page: 'you don't qualify'.

Ella-Jo Mehta

SHE

Fixture and fittings was a woman's lot
Love and obey and serve her husband's dinner hot
Produce an heir, hasn't she done well
She's only twenty, you could never tell.

She throws herself under a horse
A friend of Emily of course
With chains the protest went on
Till the light at the end of the tunnel shone.

The law had set her free
But equality was not to be
It's a man's world out there
They make the rules and that's fair.

Today sees her leading the way
But a heavy price she has to pay
Twice as hard to prove her stuff
To cut it out there, it's still rough.

In centuries to come her wisdom will be known
Love and compassion and sensitivity shown
Each person can live in harmony without war
Giving their talents to enrich the world more.

Lorraine Clarke

A SPECIAL LOVE

We have a special love we share
The two of us as one
A special love beyond compare
The difficulties we've overcome

I love you now as I did then
All those years ago
What we've been through Darling
No one will ever know

The trauma of the last year
Really took its toll
We lived with pain and fear
But we've nearly reached our goal

We've had to cope with cancer
Change we've coped with too
Will there ever be an answer?
Will they ever find something new?

The new millennium's approaching
Perhaps they'll find a cure
What a wonderful feeling
If cancer was no more

Darling the time for you was tough
You still find it hard to cope
I know the road's been very rough
But we never gave up hope

Our lives have changed forever
But you're no different now to me
We'll face this thing together
And that's how it will always be

Glenys Broxton

UNTITLED

Things have changed, unchain those links,
Remove yourselves from the kitchen sinks,
Get yourselves up out of that bed,
And the thoughts of England from your head,
Use your vote, get on your feet,
Put your cross, upon the sheet,
Raise your glass and give a cheer,
Enjoy yourselves with a pint of beer,
Get a job and share the chores,
Equal rights are now all yours!

Susan Cooper

WOMAN 2000

A woman's femininity
Was once a treasured quality,
But modern trends deny the lure
Of aspects kindly and demure.
Today's young hopefuls must comply
With feminism's jaded eye,
Or suffer the contemptuous jeers
Of brasher and less nubile peers.
Where now the dignity and grace
Once hallmarked in a lovely face
Unsullied by the curling lip
Of feminine one-upmanship?
Let woman never be denied
Equality and towering pride,
But let these benisons be more
The fruits of love than spoils of war.
May she then clarify her views
With bubbling humour, which eschews
That most unfeminine lament -
The cry of woman militant.
Millennium girls should learn to bend
Towards a less defensive trend.
A ready smile, a gleaming tress,
The gift of giving happiness.
A recipe which Eve began -
To very gently conquer man!

Joan Howes

BEST KEPT OUT OF SIGHT

What can I possibly write about men,
That's not already been written about them?
They can look smart, appear presentable,
May be introduced at a dinner table.

But all too often their bad faults appear,
Pick their noses, shove fingers in their ear.
Forget where they are, give out a large sigh,
Women do not know if to laugh or cry.

Yes ladies, men are best kept out of sight,
Not safe to take out, even for one night.

S Mullinger

A Hard Day's Work

Washing, cleaning, cooking, shopping,
A woman's work is never done,
More so in Grandma's day,
Labour saving gadgets she had none.

Washing day was a hard task,
Possing and rubbing the clothes,
Wringing them through the mangle,
Till the brows sweat ran down her nose.

Bath night involved hard labour,
A job no one would desire,
Carrying endless buckets of water,
To fill the tin bath by the fire.

Everything was lovingly polished,
Rugs shook and beaten in the yard,
The kitchen range weekly black leaded,
A woman's life indeed was hard.

Gran's hands were always busy,
Kneading dough for home-baked bread,
Making nourishing meals for her family,
Knitting, sewing, before retiring to bed.

Modern day woman still toils hard,
To earn life's luxuries she works
On returning home her chores await,
Housewifery, she will not shirk,

With the aid of modern appliances,
Microwaves, auto-washers and vacs,
Hubby may scoff, tell her life's easy,
But could he cope with her tasks?

What will the new millennium bring?
For hard working women it won't change a thing.

Barbara Sowden

A WOMAN'S ROLE

A woman's place is in the home
Or so I've heard it said
Whoever said it got it wrong
For that idea's quite dead.
A woman's work is never done
She toils from dawn till night
She's mother, cook and cleaner
And keeps the home just right.
She's chauffeur for her kids to school
She shops for food to feed them
Then goes to work to get some cash
Amid the work force mayhem.
She works in office or in shop
In factory or in school
She can be carer, doctor, nurse
But certainly no fool.

Gone are the days when she sat at home
In a role so clearly stated
Obeying her lord and master
The man to whom she was mated.
A woman now has a mind of her own
She knows what she wants from life
She wants the best for her family
And still wants to be a good wife.
A woman in love will support her man
To try and help him as much as she can.
But she'll have that independent streak
She'll be her own woman - in feminine peak.

E Wilcox

THE WAY IN THE FUTURE

Women of the world today
   Have a special role to play
With life so busy and hurried
   Hopes for the future must not be buried

Through all the ages we learn
   On history book pages
Women have flourished
   Throughout the world in all its stages

As we approach the year 2000
   With every day life updated
We can hope and pray
   To banish all hatred

Women must in 2000
   Make sure the children understand
That the way ahead
   Is to bring peace to our land

So women of the world unite
   Making certain in the year 2000
The role we play
   Will enrich the future in every way

Sheila Briggs

SILENT NO MORE

No more are we little ladies
Always knowing our place
Used, abused and ridiculed
The lesser of the human race

Our place was in the home
With ordered duties for the day
While the man went out to work
We were never allowed a say

Always doing what was expected of us
No identity, just housekeeper, wife, mother
Not heard of to voice an opinion
No one listened or cared if we did, one way or the other

But we've evolved from year to year
By pushing forward, standing our ground
Doing things that a 100 years ago were unheard of
No more, are we duty bound

We vote, work, drive, speak, we're equal, well almost
We have nights out, whilst the man stays at home
We've created new beings, called househusbands
Who cook and clean, and don't mind being left alone

The modern woman still has her roles in life
Mother, wife etc, but with a name
Never looking back to how things were in yesteryears
Woman won't go there again

Over the years women have earned identity
Lost is the role of a human afraid to speak out
We've gained strength and independence
Proving to man, what we're all about

2000, things will probably stay the same more or less
But given another 100 years, it'll be man who wears a dress

Petina Rosina Anderson

THE MILLENNIUM WOMAN - AN IMPOSSIBLE DREAM?

The millennium woman, what can that mean?
A distinguished figure or an impossible dream?
A mother of kindness, a lady of leisure
A woman of work, a woman of pleasure
From boardroom to priesthood, from model to scholar
What ever vocation that women will follow
To triumph above obstacles and barriers of power
To juggle commitments, to smile with endeavour

Back seats disregarded, to the ones with the dream
A dream of persistence, of merit and strife
Which sometimes with effort, can be achieved by a wife
To ponder and mull is never enough
The anger for freedom is a definite must
The fight is courageous, with valour and pain
But never will women be treated the same
As past life has taught them, by women of strong
The women who win are the women with tongue

The voice of an angel, the wrath of a whore
The tone of compassion, the indelible roar
A woman of substance, of faith within life
A woman whose future is determined by might
What more can a woman hope to achieve?
Than the hope of reality of their impossible dream
A dream of equality and height amongst men
Who at one time dismissed them as second to them
The millennium woman will no longer abstain
The millennium woman will year 2000 remain

Jan Le Bihan Panter

THE 2000 WOMAN

Woman synonymous with second class citizen
Once downtrodden without status or hope
Bearing children who often died
And working so hard to survive

Woman not consulted or respected
Often used and abused by men
No voice - no vote - no self esteem
But still the spirit survived

Woman so brave slowly revolted
Fought for a place of their own
Encouraged each other to take and grasp
What was theirs - their right to take

Woman now in places of respect
With learning gained equality
Enjoyed at last the right to speak
The right to contribute

Forward now into an exciting century
Of possibilities and responsibilities
Fuelled on to what was so hard fought for
Into a new millennium

Edna D'Lima

THAT TIME OF THE MONTH (MILLENNIUM OR NOT . . .)

Wrapped up in anger
My personality changed
Mind on edge
My body feels strange
Fat and ugly
Spots on my face
Confidence gone
Splitting headaches

Senselessly sensitive
Tired and stressed
Highly creative
Nothing suppressed
Breasts tender and swollen
No patience at all
Urgently horny
Nerves raw

Cry about nothing
Stuck in a rut
Self absorbed
I finally see . . .
Poor me
Poor me
I've got
PMT

Miranda Rook

THEN AND NOW

Monday was the washing day,
Crystals in the tub.
Tuesday was the ironing day,
Press and sweat and rub.
Wednesday was the cleaning day,
Tea leaves spread about,
Thursday was another day,
Of clean and cook and shout!
Friday was the pay day,
Hope he had a job!
Weekends were our special time,
With good food on the hob.

Driving through the rush hour,
Planning for the meeting.
Keeping to the guidelines,
Thinking of the seating.
Hoping that the nanny,
Was caring for the kids.
Hoping that the big boss,
Was going to win the bids.
Thinking of the shopping,
Thinking of a meal.
Wondering 'bout my life plan,
Thinking of the deal.

Hope I win the lottery,
Hope it's all worthwhile.
Wonder what it's all about,
Drive another mile.

Marily McCann

WOMAN'S WORDS

As I sit here with thoughts of a wonderful woman, my mother,
Her tales of how things were in her young days,
How things were done in so many different ways.
Clean white starched pinafores were order of the day,
Trotting off to school, singing all the way,
Home again at the end of the day,
To do some chores to earn your half penny pay.
As soon as age came around, when you could go your adult way,
Off to the factory to earn a bigger pay.
So different from the woman of today,
Doctors, teachers, preachers, not a pinafore, slate or chalk.
Just computers, tele-fax, shopping on the net,
But I'm one of the 'old ones', we're just as happy as the
                                           present 'jet set'.

S Storey

HYSTERECTOMY

I haven't got a garden, but always there
Are flowers in my rooms. They remind me of
Children, their scents leaping up at me when
I come in. The personality of their colours
Is brash and bright. I love them on the sills,
Around the bed, and even on the floor.
They can distract me from almost anything.

I let the first one in about ten thirty.
Three more before a regular. He keeps
His socks on and talks of his mother. She'll
Get the Queen's telegram next year, and that,
I hear, as the chrysanthemums grow taller,
After a life working her fingers to the bone.
He takes his pleasure, then tells me after, he
Could never leave her. His hair's lank, his palms
Are sweaty, and when I take his money, there's
A look in his eye that says he's a bully.

The street's a long way down. He's let across
A road awash with cars, and lorries marked
Boots, W H Smith, Tesco. Then he's lost
At last, and I resume my work. My smile
Has improved since when I was at Do-It-All.
But my dreams have stayed much the same. Well,
I'll have my womb back when I'm rich enough . . .

I throw out the dead heads and condoms, pour
A glass of wine and listen to Mozart. All
Night I'll have just sweet air for company.

Chloe Loe

FEEDING MY SOUL

I needed to find time
I needed to find space
In my life
Again
To feed my soul
With ingredients
It once had
With ingredients
It was now starved of
Overtime
Neglect crept in
Neglect found itself a home
A home where little Zahida grew

Z Darr

IMAGINE

I try to imagine what life would be like
To turn back the clock a century ago,
Wearing long dresses to clean out the fire,
Polishing and dusting the wooden floors.

I try to imagine Monday morning washing
Water so cold in a big metal tub,
Scrubbing so hard the dirt from the clothes,
Hands are quite red and feeling so sore.

Thank goodness for jeans and sensible clothes
Hooray, for electricity to light up my fire,
To hoover the carpet laid on the floor,
Washing the clothes in an electric machine.

Imagine a computer fixed in my home
Press of a button, work is all done.
Computerised clothes that fit like a glove,
Press of a button, I am all clothed.

Dee Twomey

MILLENNIUM WOMAN

With her feet she can travel,
Explore and be free.
Nothing can hold her back.
No one can push her forward.

On her back she can carry
Heavy loads, heavy burdens.
Her work is her life.
Her home is her world.

With her arms she embraces
With love and with warmth.
She can have what she needs.
She can keep what she loves.

With her mouth she can laugh,
Speak her mind, tell the truth.
She will have reason to smile.
She will have no need to frown.

With her ears she shall hear
Good news and kinds words.
She will listen and learn.
She will hear and be heard.

And with her mind she will conquer,
Defeat problems, become stronger.
Her mind has no limits.
Her thoughts are her power.

Susan M Brown

What It Will Mean To Women In The Year 2000

Freedom

The year 2000 will see the smaller family unit
Leaving time to taste the pleasures of the world

The age of computer technology - helping young and old

Medicine

Medical progress has taken a giant step - and will go on doing so
People will have longer lives with medical advances

Education

Enables women to choose their career

The year 2000 is beyond imagination - anything can happen
Wonderful things have been achieved

Men will have their place - they will now look up to us

And to achieve all this we must not let God stray from our lives

Kindness, not greed will conquer

We look up to all clever people - our lives are in their hands

We look forward to the spring taking our breath away
With all the beauty it has to offer

Memories we must put in the past
Together with the outgoing 1000 years
It has been a time for sadness

However the twentieth century
Leading to the millennium

It will be our finest hour

Frances Abrahart

THE LINK

Great Grandmother fled from a hostile land
To safety here - married an Englishman.
Never mastered the language,
Was often misunderstood,
But everyone acknowledged
Her love for her children.

Grandmother's place was in the home.
Then, conflict carrying off the men,
She rolled up her sleeves for the war effort.
Forced to stop work when the soldiers returned,
She never gave up
Loving her children.

Mother brought up her family;
Watched despairing as one child died.
Going to University, she
Became a doctor of philosophy,
But her highest honour
Was the love of her children.

Daughter, granddaughter, the line marches on
Who can predict how their lives will unfold.
Mountaineer, pilot, astronaut -
The sky's the limit, perhaps beyond.
But the thread that binds their past and their future
Is women's enduring love for their children.

Joan Burdon

WOMAN OF SUBSTANCE

Where did they come from, and where are they going,
Those women of substance, who once were unknown,
They are now stepping out, in this world that we know,
Taking positions of power as they go.

Once, held down by the masculine thumb,
Prevented from having their say,
Those women of substance fought hard to be heard,
And their patience and struggle did pay.

Their place in the background, to be seen but not heard,
Made them slaves to great masculine power,
But with courage they fought, and are seen now and heard,
And great wisdom on others they shower.

From far in the background of silence they came,
To speak with great wisdom and grace,
They've enabled all women to fight and achieve,
And yield power at a fast running pace.

Opportunities now for women are there,
To work now as equals and share,
Positions or power only once held by men,
Now at last our society's fair.

Once treated like slaves, the woman rebelled,
Changing history once and for all,
Determined they were, as they fought for their rights,
Now as equals they stand proud and tall.

Marjory Davidson

LET US WOMEN HAVE OUR SAY!

Hearing, 'It's a man's world'
Makes me so, so mad!
(Not that I'm saying
Men are all that bad!)
In some ways I rather like them,
They can be a lot of fun.
'Til they hand you their sweaty clothes to wash,
When coming home from a run.
But why should our world
Be dominated by men?
And why should women fit the role
Of a homely mother hen?
Women are just as able,
In the working world.
So why does even screaming
Make our voices somehow not heard?
I sure do love being a woman,
But I feel that I must say,
We never get a proper chance
To prove we can do things our way!
We want a chance of equality,
Not just staying in the home.
So stop being dated and listen,
We want status of our own!

Donna Whalley

REVERSAL

I'm, sending you an e-mail - couldn't get you on the phone
Know you'll switch on the computer as soon as you get home

The golf and lunch dragged on and on - the presentation it was slow
Yes- I will be home late again tonight - don't say it - yes - I know

I know it's my turn for the brownie run - and put the kids to bed
But if only you knew how stressed I am
And what's going through my head

I know I missed *Sainsbury's* night last week
I'll take my turn don't worry
I can't continue at this rate
It's just hurry - hurry - hurry

I'll see you later - about ten
Yes - things will be alright
Oh God - It's Wednesday - can you please
Remember to tape the big fight

When I get in - don't give me hassle
Please - for once - just try to be fair
I'll make it up to you this weekend
Lots of love and kisses
Claire

Frances Rimmington

THE EMERGENCE

The girl unfolds
into a woman,
and the change
is marked
deep, deep,
within.
The arms of
the women
and the generations
roll back
to Mother Nature
and God.
God
looks at his creation
and loves
what he sees.

Angela Patchett

FRIDAY 6TH NOVEMBER 1998

If they were going to come,
It would be on a night like this.
What with the flashes and bangs of fireworks
Their 'all-clear' signal to the mother ship
Would probably go unnoticed.

You can smell the stars tonight,
And the clear sky and a bonfire,
And there's enough coldness
To prickle the hairs on the back of your neck
(If you move too much or think too hard.)

(The rustling in the dead leaves
Is *probably* just a rat
Or the evening breeze.
It really *isn't* likely to be them
Scuffling out of sight.

Would they hide in ditches,
Watching us pass by, and learning?
They're probably hanging around in car parks,
Looking like people I know.
That's what I'd do if I were them.)

I saw them tonight.
Six bright stars in a straight line,
Sliding through the sky towards the moon.
And I know they saw me watching them,
Because the lights faded gently

                              into nothing.

A Savage

FORBIDDEN LOVE

As the room plunges into darkness
All thoughts fade from her mind.
Her pulse quickens,
As she waits for the earth to move.

Tears fall heavily onto white sheets,
Releasing hidden emotions.

The innocence is gone
Erased in a clumsy moment of passion.
The key is cast and the earth
Remains still.

Vanessa Wells

FALLEN

Sycamore butterfly seeds
wing spirally away
resisting air.

Flying colours hold
brief eminence within
my languid stare.

October, lashing wind
destroys mosaic finery;
life falling spare.

Judith Thomas

MILLENNIUM FEVER

The sun, moon and stars dance to the music of the spheres.
They give light and love to planet Earth,
Our home for a brief span.
The awesome eclipse gives us a glimpse of wonder
and exacting precision uniting in balance and harmony.
Each soul joined together sharing this momentous experience.
Our contribution of technological dreams in stark reality we
venture into realms unknown,
With our gods we strive to believe in our inner worlds.
The millennium to many gave time to reflect and pause,
To nourish our planet with equanimity for all living beings,
We must strive onwards in each moment to cherish this precious life.
What we give will be returned in abundance, we hold the future
in our hands.

Olivia Hicks

SHE

She, in a man's world,
Or, so it is called,
Women can do a grand job,
With energy, and daily drive,
As time draws near,
For the millennium year,
Survival that's what it is
All about.
Everyone will be alright,
Imagine the parties on the
Eve of millennium night.
Yes it is fair, with a little
Thought everyone will care.
Celebration, across the nation,
A way forward to believe,
Doing everything is what
Women can achieve.

Caroline Janney

LIBERATED WOMEN

We've approached the year 2000
And we're in the early days
Let us remember the Suffragettes
For whom we have great praise

They chained themselves to railings
Suffered for their cause
To liberate us women
They broke so many laws

They got us a job and gave us a vote
So that we could equal men
We must make sure that this century
Does not see us downtrodden again

Since then we've had a lady PM
And a female astronaut
We've served in the Armed Forces
And beside the men we've fought

We're not now chained to railings
Or the kitchen sink
You poor men can't burn your bras
So have another think

So do what you do best always
Run off to the pub
But remember the days have long since gone
When we stayed up to cook your grub

No longer are we the *weaker sex*
We're stronger than you men
So to the Suffragettes of long ago
We must always remember them

Vera Blaylock

UNTITLED

I can recall those long, hazy summer evenings
when love hung heavy from every bough,
dripping,
oozing with the scents and tastes of summer fruit
and cooling wine.
There I discovered love and felt once more like a child,
protected by my mother's sweet caress.

Too soon my love, the summer crept away,
unnoticed,
leaving love naked to the bitterest winter, and now,
forgotten fruit oh sumptuous forbidden fruit, lies sparse in fields
of sodden earth where skeleton trees await rebirth.
But whilst I'm sitting here my love with thoughts of days gone by,
I'll hold a heavy heart my love and breathe a tearful sigh.
I often wonder if, my love,
each dark and restless night, the future holds a time for us,
one endless summer night?

Emma Stringfellow

No Proper Job?

'Do you have a job,' they say.
'What do you do at home all day?'
'Oh, nothing much, I clean and cook,
Spend hours seeing how I look.'
'You don't do any work all week,
Are your days not dull and bleak?
You don't temp, not just some hours?'
'No, I walk the dog and do the flowers,
I bake a cake for the charity stall,
My life is not dull or bleak at all.
I wash and iron and do the dishes,
I make the beds and feed the fishes.
I am a teacher, nurse and friend,
A quite fulfilling day I spend.
Husband and children are my life,
It's a full-time job with three under five!'

Maria Entecott

A HUNDRED YEARS OF WOMEN'S LIVES

Women's lives have changed since then!
Perhaps in more ways than for men!
Their clothes were long, and dark and neat,
Which covered them from neck to feet.
Their hair grew long, and piled up high,
No perms, nor short cut styles to try!
Most of the women when they wed
Stayed at home, to work instead.
There were unending tasks to do,
No modern machines to see them through,
The washing took at least three days,
With boiling and old-fashioned ways.
They cooked and baked and made their bread,
On an old-fashioned range, instead!
Entertainment was simple in their day,
No TV, radio or CDs to play!
Sing-songs round the piano, and card games too
Helped to see their evenings through.
They read a lot, and books might tell
How they should vote, like men as well.
Most husbands *told* them what they'd decided,
So women's views were much derided!
But equality would be years away,
Until we come to lives today.
Now, we are free to travel and roam,
But *then*, most took holidays near to home.
Now, despite inventions of every kind,
We find it difficult to unwind!
They were more contented then, I fear,
Than we are in this millennium year!

Joyce Reynolds

NINETIES WOMAN

She runs a business, runs a home
and runs her children to their school.
Each day is all a frantic dash
to beat the clock while staying cool.

At work she's in complete control -
decisions made and contracts signed.
She has her finger on the pulse -
A model of new womankind.

With trading finished for the day
the time has come to switch her mind
to dinner and her family's needs.
Each segment of each day defined.

At home she isn't quite so sure
that she has got the upper hand.
The chores are never-ending, but
this is the life that she had planned.

And when at last she gets to bed,
though tired to death, sleep will not come.
She thinks about the future and
life in the new millennium.

Another year won't bring much change.
In essence things will stay the same.
She'll keep her job, her boys will grow.
Their happiness always her aim.

She'll have to race to beat the clock
that measures out the daily hours,
but we all know that working mums
are blessed with superhuman powers!

Patricia Farley

PROGRESS

1960s

Eternal housework,
Children fight, mothers sigh -
Whole years roll slowly by.

1990s

Housework quickly done,
Children grown, long since flown -
No need for sighs,
Freedom's now the golden prize.

Eileen M Lodge

THE END OF AN ERA

I rock to and fro in my rocking chair
All my memories I can remember thee
As I wait for the clock to strike midnight
My eyes now misty with my failing sight

I reminisce with a smile of those years
Tinged with laughter and sometimes tears
A bride so young barely a child
At times I was lonely sometimes wild

We married when I was barely seventeen
But my man was a diamond and ever so keen
Oh how we loved to spin and to dance
Twirling, swirling like in a trance

The sands of time when he was mine
We matured together like a good fine wine
Not much money but we had such fun
Now this century is almost done

We had no electricity but candles were lit
Huddled by our log fire we would sit
No television then so we'd take early nights
Our eager passions were our delights

I rock and smile as the clock ticks by
I am ready to go now I'm ready to die
The changes in the future I will not see
For the millennium a spirit I'll be

I close my eyes as I can see his face
Waiting for me with dignity and grace
The clock strikes midnight the end is mine
For the millennium I'll wake up in another time

Lannette Lusk

THE MILLENNIUM WOMAN

The millennium woman
Should not just be able
To turn heads
Like a porcelain doll
But to challenge minds
With a wit so sharp
It could slice through
Prejudice and old ideas
Leaving them ripped
And disregarded.

The millennium woman
Should not insult
Those who have gone before
Those who cried out
With shrill voices
For change, and freedom
Cries which shattered
Much more than glass
But the arrogance
Of previous thought.

The millennium woman
Should not be complacent
And bask in the sunlight
That other women have set
A flame that must never die
She should strive
For freedom of mind
And spirit
Into the millennium
Not forgetting the past.

Judith Kemp

THE BUTTERFLY - REBIRTH

The Butterfly that became a beautiful memory
Suddenly . . . just like the phoenix arises from her ashes.
Slowly and gradually she repairs herself
Her wings enmeshing and bonding together
Becoming sturdy and strong.
No longer the fragile, delicate creature.
No longer the social butterfly
Her flight is solo
She flies and soars freely and independently into the blue sky.
Towards sunshine and light
Towards the warmth
Her healing almost complete
What had become the ending
Has now become . . . the beginning . . .

Marilyn D Bowerbank

SIXTY MILES

Sixty miles away
my sister aches,
cramped with pain and
wet with tears
and sickness biting deeply
into her very being.

Sixty miles away
I hold the telephone
and cry silently,
as my sister cries,
aching with pain
she cannot help but taste.

She cannot help but taste the pain.
Friends have fed her venom -
A vile bile surging through her fragile veins

and sixty miles away
I have no antidote but experience.
My past is no tonic
for her present
and now I am bruised
by our difference.

Fiona Louise Brice

HOW WOULD IT FEEL?

How would it feel, I wonder, to go back 30 years,
When if you held a job down
To be redundant held no fears?

The economy was booming, you could pick and choose
If you had an education,
You really couldn't lose.

The workplace then was happy, a job was held for life,
You didn't have to worry -
Or rely upon the wife.

To work hard was second nature, and no one tried to skive,
To work then was a pleasure,
You didn't toil to stay alive.

These days the threat hangs over every person who's employed,
Any news that breaks tomorrow
May get the stock market annoyed.

Then jobs go out the window and those left employed do even more,
They take on the tasks of workmates
Who've just been shown the door.

The working week's expanding, it now spans seven days,
And people shop upon the Sabbath
Which never ceases to amaze.

Where are the family values?
That one day when all can rest?
When those who work on Sundays
Can in their family's lives invest?

How would it feel I wonder to go back 30 years
When almost everyone was working
And to be redundant held no fears?

Gillian Brion

LOVE'S YOUNG DREAM

I remember when we fed each other squares of chocolate
Sitting together on our favourite park bench
And stealing kisses shyly on the corners of our mouths
You picked me a bunch of wild flowers
Down by the old railway cutting
A beautiful gift, full of colour and scent
The blue of the cornflowers like your eyes
So dazzling, full of sweet intent
I loved you so much when you smiled
And I loved you even more with your arm around my shoulders
So snug in the cinema
With the crinkle of our large bag of Maltesers
Making us giggle, while we were tutted at
When you met me after school, I'd changed from sensible flat shoes
To three and a half inch platforms
Just to be told you'd seen me in my flatties
From your seat on the bus that morning!
But you said you loved me whatever I wore on my feet
We were love's young dream 'til the adults woke us
But the memories will always make me smile.

Lynda Mullarkey Wood

IN HIDING

In our waking
We saw the sun
Through cracks and slits
In our days
We smelled stale dust
And waste
And misered out
Our scraps of food
And all the while
The while the hunger gnawed
And the fear clenched.

In our sleep
We heard the crunch
Of boots on gravel
In our dreams
They looked for bicycles
And razor blades
Or anything or anyone
That could be hiding
And all the while
The while the hunger gnawed
And the fear clenched.

We woke each day
And found our sleep
Was waking
And our dreams
Reality.

Sylvia Goodman

AWAKE

Trees stand black at dawn;
Waving coldly under a warming sky.
Houses stand irrelevant to Nature's task,
Sleep seeping from cracks in the concrete.

Time edges nearer to day,
Awakening colour and drawing shapes.
Familiarity becoming common once again,
Unidentifying the strange that was dark.

Separating day from night;
Sun changing shifts with moon.
And people become simple when awake;
The complexity of dreams now far away.

The trees wave green against the sky;
Artistic blue with summer.
Curtains are drawn inelegantly,
And consciousness makes the day what it is.

Caz Maughan

GIRL POWER

Scrubbing and cleaning the kitchen floor,
ready for her man as he opens the door.
Food on the table piping hot,
she waits behind for him to have his lot.
She fills the tub next to the fire,
then waits for the nod so she can retire.
Up at dawn preparing another day,
she dreams and wishes women could have a say.
One woman listened and heard their plights,
she was Mrs Pankhurst who fought for women's rights.
Times have changed, the year two thousand is near,
Girl Power Rules we hear a cheer.

Suzanne Watson

SUNSET

She lifted her face to the setting sun's rays
Enjoying the warmth of those late summer days
And she thought of her youth as both wife and mother
The struggles and worries. She had known no other
The babies came quickly. Seven all told
But three bairns died when only days old.
Her marriage began with such love and hope
Too soon she was left on her own to cope.
There were sticks to chop and coals to carry
Fires to be lit. No time to tarry,
The copper wash boiler gave off clouds of steam
And she peered through the mist in search of her dream
Like her mother before her dream bubbles had burst
No matter how weary the children came first.
Through bombings and blackouts fighting hunger and tears
She sheltered her wee ones, made light of their fears.
A wraith of the man she had loved and wed
Lay wounded and bandaged in a hospital bed
She called to her children at the ward door
'This man is your father' and she cried no more.
Those days were gone now. She was left with the sadness
That so many memories had so little gladness,
She clasped worn hands and began to pray
As she watched the sunset at the end of the day.

Siné Machir

A Woman's Work

Women through the centuries
had a set role to play
in giving birth to children
and running the home all day

The suffragettes then rallied
giving forth the cry
'We have a right to vote
and for this we're prepared to die'

At last some men did notice
women's value in the war
and began to reconsider
what they were fighting for

Little by little the men gave way
and acknowledged a woman's right
to have a say all of her own
regardless of gender or might

Equality in the workplace
came about with a dual aim
giving women an alternative
and the chance to earn the same

With the millennium finally here
women struggle to balance life
between a working mother
or that of a traditional wife

Nicola Martin

POTTED CYCLAMENS

A communion cup held upside down
which in normal circumstances
would be empty
yet
still miraculously filled with the heady wine
of air, space, light and silence.

But wings pathetically poised as though on the brink of flight
pinned down in a pot
and placed in a cloistered atmosphere
are grounded.

Some spilt upon a carpet
faintly reminiscent of brown earth and green grass
like a cloud of discarded petticoats thrown off
during an ecstatic night of revelries
held long ago in some distant place
full of air, space, light and silence.

And even as I watch
those buds still closed and furled
in the fastened shape of fine ladies' parasols
suddenly begin to furiously uncurl
as if with one thought only
that those delicate petalled parachutes
may propel them
away from our perturbed world
to taste again the heady wine of communion
with air, space, light and silence.

Judith Garrett

UNITY'S AMAZON QUEEN

(Dedicated to Una Brandon-Jones, one of Unity Theatre's most extraordinary members)

Our ageing Amazon Queen,
Stalwart of the left-wing scene,
Leaning on her blackened cane,
Moving ma-jesti-cally,
Down a theatre's staircase,
Yet her spirit does not wane.

Years back in Theatre Group,
This actress and director,
And feminist songwriter,
Displayed her *Women's Lib* ways,
As she lead *The Amazons,*
An all female revue troupe.

A magnificently tall,
Powerful old warrior,
In showbiz's crown a jewel
Though she is over eighty,
She's a sparky old lady,
With character in her face.

Her white hair swept back from:
Clear, grey, narrow, bright eyes,
Sparkling with encouragement,
For these acting gals and guys,
Since her *Unity* days
She's disliked waste of talent.

And continuing her flow,
Up on stage, heading the show,
Is her striking daughter,
A wild redheaded creature,
Taking her place in the team,
Another Amazon Queen?

Emma Dorothy Shane

WASHING IN THE MORNING

Apply and lather,
The yellow smear of sticky soap.
The gradual whitening over grey
Like the beginning of a new dawn.
A pool of water rippling with suds.

Immerse the cloth,
Holding it under the surface,
Suffocating the last bubble of air,
Plunging hands into every hidden fold,
Pounding and squeezing, raising a storm.

Drain dirty water,
Gurgling, a creamy whirlpool.
Suck the last trace of reality
Into screaming oblivion.
Spiralling thoughts and senses reel.

Turn on the taps,
A cascade of fresh liquid,
Rushing, the climax of sinful ecstasy.
Erasing the shame and lies that taint
Their virgin white appearance.

Clean bedsheets.

D G Niyadurupola

THE MOTH

The moth dances madly around the night lamp's glow,
As though
In that one burning centre
All hope, all joy, all life exist;
So helpless love,
Aware, yet powerless to resist.

See the frantic flutter of the soft wings,
Body clings
Ungainly, as though to oppose
The masochistic plunge, the spurning;
So prescience, pride,
Surrenders all to the body's yearning.

Useless to prevent the certain fate,
Too late;
The heedless flight is over,
And all hope, all joy, all life is done.
Turn out the light
Now that my love has gone.

Thia Sellens

LIFE VS LIFE

Candles glow within the soul,
Goodness of life burns so strong.
The eyes have seen
And mouths have brought,
The breath alight,
The candle taught.
Through life the candle's gone
and still the empty shell lives on.
It moves with control ahead.
The eyes that saw
and mouth that brought,
The breath so dear
and now has caught,
the candle as it once began,
with the soul that sprightly sang.
The song of life that still is heard,
by those who hold the candle high,
Proud to see the tears that cry.

Hollie Simmons

REFLECTIONS

'This is me!' she cried
As she threw the mirror,
It exploded into a thousand shards
And a slither lodged in his liver.

Like a house of cards
Dismissed by Alice
He collapsed in her wake.

Tomorrow was hers
As she looked in the mirror
And her child appeared
At her shoulder
To remind her
That the world is full of rules
And tomorrow
Belongs to the young
And the optimistic.

'This was me!' she cried
And she smashed the mirror
And cut her wrist -
By mistake . . . ?

J H Keers

SOUL DANCE

I am the dream of me

creating in form

wonders that I am

from mists

to earth

Jackie Draysey

MILLENNIUM LULLABY

Darling daughter, sleeping softly,
Clock ticking on the wall,
You are growing faster daily,
Babyhood takes no time at all.

As you age what will life bring you?
The world is an oyster for my pearl,
Increased knowledge brings harder decisions,
Your mind will be in a constant whirl.

What job will you do as computers take over?
Where will you live as barriers come down?
Will you get married and stay home with your babies?
Or will you become the career girl about town?

What will you wear when you go out for the evening?
Where will you meet the man of your dreams?
Will you be able to have dinner in Sydney,
When you fancy a change of scene?

Will you grow your own children in test tubes?
Will pregnancy and childbirth be a thing of the past?
How long will you live when the medics find the answers,
To making your health and beauty last?

I wish you well as we begin the new millennium,
You awake, with cherub cheeks flushed and pink,
Oh my beautiful daughter,
I hope the future is less confusing than I think.

Fleur Whiteman

HIATUS

In the heart of the wind
        there is a silence,

In the moment of rainfall
        there is a stillness,

A pause
        for breath,

A space
        for catching up

with what is lost
in the burl
of staying alive.

Beth Short

OUR HUMBLE JUMBLE

The trestles are set, the clothes piled high
And the bric-a-brac is by the door.
Boots and shoes are over to the left
And an old TV sits near a drawer.

We've lampshades and teapots
And old books by the score,
Plus a frayed wicker chair
Sits forsaken on the floor.

A dented whistling kettle
Pedal bin and three-wheeled skate
Mournfully rest, beside
a red milk crate.

A table of mahogany
Leans against the stage,
And on the top resplendent
Is an old bird cage.

Where we have the toys and clocks
And bits and bobs of china,
Is a little dog with just one ear
The lady said was *'Designer'*.

Now we're ready with our goodies
Out-of-date and out of style.
So, is everybody ready
By their nominated pile?

Unlock the door now girls, let's
Welcome everyone.
Welcome to our jumble sale
Where everything's homespun.

Pamela Sears

A Cry From A Nursing Home, Or A Peep Into The Future?

Now I am so much older
My memory is not the same.
I am sure I know who you are
But I cannot recall your name.
My love for you is just as deep
And always will be that way.
Inside my heart I am just the same,
It is my mind that is fading away.

Surely this place is not my home
Where is my favourite chair?
Who are those people, so like me?
What are they doing there?
Everything is so confusing,
Is it meant to be this way?
Have I always lived like this?
Please, will it end one day?

Did I dream a warm sensation
As you held me in your embrace?
Could that have been your gentle tear
Which landed on my face?
My memories fade so quickly,
But I am sure you did hold me tight
And gave me just a tiny kiss
As you whispered a last 'Goodnight.'

J Stevens

SOMERSET LANDSCAPE SYMPHONY

The East wind picks up, frolics in grasses,
Brushing dead brittle whitened stems
With a swishing sound that swiftly passes
Whispering across fields - a hymn
Of winter. Heavy early morning mist
Persists, menacing and massing
Cold clinging on far frosted hills, resists
Sun that targets fir trees, dressing
An overnight counterpane with pale beams.
River is still - sheeted thin ice -
No longer fretting its bank, curves and gleams
A silver strand in the distance.
Savour this fair landscape on such a day
And dare who will to call it grey.

Rosemary Langdon

MY DREAM LOVER

The moon rode high in a velvet sky
The night wind stirred the trees
As I walked in the scented garden
My lover came to me

He was bronzed and he was handsome
And as he kissed my hand and bowed
Curls as soft as a raven's wing
Tumbled over his brow.

He gently pulled me to him
Encircling me in his arms
My heart was wildly beating
As I surrendered to his charms

He whispered softly in my ear
Of the love that he was feeling
His lips met mine in a sensuous kiss
That sent my senses reeling

A night owl hooted softly
As we slid slowly to the ground
I lay entwined in his embrace
And in a sea of feeling drowned

He ran his fingers through my hair
His dark brown eyes a-gleaming
And then I woke up with a start
Alas! I was only dreaming.

Freda Pilton

GOING HOME

A foot on the platform;
A foot on the train;
Trying to escape
My ball and chain.

A smoky seat;
A man with no name;
The silence does nothing
To ease my pain.

An unknown village;
A stuttering drain;
It all seems to change
But my feelings are the same.

The shudder of the engines;
The patter of the rain;
I don't really want to do this
I'm coming home again.

Alight at the next platform;
A place called 'Misty Maine';
I cross the dusty tracks
And catch the return train.

The acrid stench of metal;
The sound of people's pain;
I crawl out of the wreckage
And try to clear my brain.

The warmth of fire inviting;
And rest appears the same;
I want to go to sleep, now
And stop this screaming pain.

My eyes are feeling heavy,
But I'll soon be home again . . .

Suie Nettle

THE CHEAT

He sat by himself
Pressed into his seat
At the back of the class
Huddled
Crumpled
Alone.

His dark eyes
Were shaped into small protective slits
As if to shut out
This world
He faced
Alone.

He did not speak
Or laugh
Or throw paper
Across the class
Earning my reprimands
With confident abandon
As other children did.

He held his pen
Fingers cramped
Knuckles white
Head crushed down
Neck pushed into
His shoulders
Ashamed
Alone.

His report said
'Papers torn up
He cheated'
It did not say
Mother dead
Father in prison
Child in care
Twelve years old
Facing the world
Alone.

Mary Howell

A FORGOTTEN LOVE SONG

I'm calling out your name, but you never hear
I'm standing right beside you but you don't even know
Your mind's so far away although your body's so near
And I can feel you beginning to let go
You might as well be halfway across the world from me
You may have forgotten you once saw what I see
But I don't want to lose you now
If there's still a chance for us somehow

Or are we just drifting, drifting away?
Like a leaf in the breeze, or a rose in the sea
Like a snowfall in spring, and these words that I sing
Drifting away, in the dream of brighter days
In the dream of brighter days.

We used to be so close, but now you're so far from me
Well maybe I was never quite what you wanted me to be
And I was never quite good enough for you
I'd tell you I could change in any way you want me to
But now I think it's too late, there's nothing I know how to do
It's you that has changed from the guy I once knew
Now I'm as lost as you

I'm deafened by the silence of the words you never say
I can see by the distance in your eyes that you've already gone away
Some day we'll meet again, when everything has changed
Nothing quite the same, then we'll try again

Because now we've just drifted, drifted away
Like a leaf in the breeze, or a rose in the sea
Like a snowfall in spring, and these words that I sing
Drifted away, in the dream of brighter days
In the dream of brighter days.

Adrienne M Gray

THE WIND WILL TELL

Girlfriend! Always be careful what you say
You don't know who is listening:
The wind *is!*
It carries the voice of your words
to the acutely delicate
and listening heart - and who knows!
Just who the hearer may be -
someone, you don't want our secrets spoken to

Girlfriend! The blame is with you, you spoke
and your words were carried on,
on the wings of the wind
Don't chide yourself too much
because to some hearers
your message is like an answered prayer -
it is sympathy and understanding.
But woe the naked mind, and the flattering tongue
to them, the secret of your heart
is the beat of a drum - travelling through mountains, hills and valleys

Girlfriend! Mind how you talk about things, anything
Whether it's my business or yours,
the sensitive hyper conscious heart,
whom it may concern
will hear it, for the voice of the wind
never stops talking: listen, can't you hear it
Even now?

Rosetta Stone

AROMA/ODOUR

This sweet and sensuous aroma of mine,
On this sunny morning in May,
The aroma scent smells so fine.

Beautifully coloured flowers, in a line,
Their different scents blowing around in every way,
This sweet and sensuous aroma of mine.

Sweet smells showing a sign,
A different colour for a different odour every day,
The aroma's scent smells so fine.

Out in a restaurant ready to dine,
The food is out, smelling so fine, there is nothing left to say,
This sweet and sensuous aroma of mine.

Tasty sources and French wine,
Everything is forgotten until you have to pay,
The aroma's scent smells so fine.

Many fragrant perfumes with names like Chanel Nine,
Which for the rest of the evening, the fragrance will stay.
This sweet and sensuous aroma of mine,
The aroma's scent smells so fine.

Kimberly Harries

WHAT NEXT?

We got the vote, we got the pill
but we are now waiting still
for equal pay for equal work
It's not fair that we miss the perk
of childcare for our own man's child
instead we sit here meek and mild
not forcing through the things we need
because we feel inferior, indeed
we do our best to get the deal
that will at all times mean we feel
that we should be treated with respect.
Next time we will be more direct,
not chained to railings but we will
together take action putting still
more energy into our words and feeling
that now too late, our senses reeling
we achieve success at last
and own the future not the past.

We've nearly got there, nearly won
the war that was for us begun,
by women long ago who knew
what we would be coming to.
So for our future we will fight
because we know we have the right
as marching forward we will stride
into a future where we decide
the playing field and all the pieces
merged into one until it ceases
to be a battle, for we shall have peace
and all of us one day will be at ease.

H Mander

THE CHANGING ROLE OF WOMEN

For women the last hundred years have changed
Their lives in general have been re-arranged
They now have a vote
Some suffered for that - please note
During the war they did a man's job
Which brought them in a few extra bob
Later, feminists for equality with the men
Burnt their bras now and then!
They now have the pill
Can limit their family at will
As now, a lot do not believe in marriage bliss
For them a lot of responsibility if they remain like this
In the Millennium they may shop from home
From their armchair all alone
They have their computers
Will surf the 'net'
Will rectify easily any item they forget
In the next Century
We hope and pray
It will be the fashion
To show others more compassion.

Eileen Hannah

. . . OF HUMAN KINDNESS

Just as I finished the ceiling, he looked in,
'There's no milk' he said.

An instant flash feasibility study,
persuaded me,
of the improbability
of a middle-aged
post-lactating female,
successfully breastfeeding
a pot-bellied menopausal male,
from the top rung of a stepladder.

Wickedly,
In delicious slow motion
I could see half a tin
of brilliant white matt emulsion,
(a bargain from Couglan's in Meath Street),
sail splashing through the knife-cut silence.
Couch potato 'au lait'!
Olé! Olé! Olé!

'There's money on the mantelpiece,
but don't make tea for me,' I said,

'I'm going for a pint!'

Christine Broe

NIGHTMARE

I wake up very, very slowly,
Pulling myself out of the abyss.
Scrabbling with my fingers to get hold of something tangible.
The bedside lamp.
The clock.   .
My pot of cleansing cream.
Tissues.
Something . . .
                    . . . Anything
Which will tell me I am really awake
And that that cold, dank, dreadful thing
Which slimes and slithers round my feet has gone.

I try opening my eyes,
Telling myself that the deeper than black shadow
Which never really materialised is still not lurking halfway
                                        along the landing.

But my nose tells me I can still smell *it*.

This is ridiculous.
My tight, tortured throat is only raw from a half-strangled
                                        nightmare scream.
The rest of my senses are dulled from the dream which I cannot
                                        throw off
Or are they heightened by imminent danger?
If I stretch out my hand in the dark what *will* I touch?
What *is* that faintly acrid smell?
Why *does* the dark through my open bedroom door have shape?
Why? . . . Why?

I feel sick.
Somewhere, deep between my feet and head, my heart is pounding.
I pull the clothes over my head
And I

S c r e a m m m!

Vera Davies

THERE IS NO FOOL . . .

'There is no fool
like an old fool,' she remarked,
reflecting on her narrow miss,
remembering how,
kiss by stealthy kiss,
his feet had inched their way
beneath her table,
meaning to stay.

Lost in aloneness,
she forgot;
took him back;
showed him her life's wealth,
put a ring on his finger,
gave him her hand,
and the strut of all her land.

He, willing and able,
sowed the next year's harvest yield -
dug a deep hole, made a round mound -
in a quiet spot
in Dead Men's Field.

Marcia Ascott

FEMME FATALE
(Whisker)

Thistledown of angel white
Sapphire jewels, ice-blue light.
Velvet step, gentle grace
Melting, moulding, warm embrace.

Contented slumber, sleepy haze
Basking warmth, timeless days.
Lazy stretch, sunlit beams
Curling, coiling, carefree dreams.

Gentle lamb now no more
Glinting eye, needled paw.
Deadly silence, stealthy gait
Alter ego, hidden trait.

Leopard, tiger, predatory queen
Sinews taut, eyes a'gleam.
Eager ebullience, merciless fun
Loaded pounce from triggered gun.

Home return, loving pet
Crystal conscience, no regret.
Serenely sleeping gentle lamb
Angelic demon, femme fatale.

Alison R E Langley

SANITY RESTORED

(Following an episode of Manic Depressive Illness)

White linen cool, their presence
Speaks of calm so long a stranger
When the deep pool abandoned me
Tranquillity
Bled into artesian wells
In some far-off corner

Clotted thoughts caught unawares
In tangled membranes
Killed reason and all recognition
Pulled by the visions
I hurtled on to touch
Thick-coated panes in royal hues
Molten purple; viscous reds
In vivid merger coursing

Clarity lost, my tired eyes were fixed
Held captive upon stained glass
Depicting agony in searing heat
Conjoined rapture and terror
Fuelled my bid
To save those lives imprisoned within
For I alone foresaw the savagery to come
The dénouement of madness brewing

Yet now I rest, bathed in soft morning
And smile at you across white lilies and cream roses
You perch with coffee mug in hand, relaxed
Once more my senses and perception
Waltz to Life's familiar tune
I am 'home' again, for now.

Kate Tavener

ATTITUDE

Impatient voice intolerant attitude
I am demeaned, no longer commanding respect,
Too old to work or be a useful citizen
Condemned to be talked down to.
Or treated like a child who doesn't understand
Simple things explained, painstakingly by strangers
Why? Could it be because my hair is white
Or because comprehension is sometimes slow?
Not because my brain is -
No, just not hearing when words are spoken quickly
Words run into one another
Like paint put on too soon, runs together and is blurred
Embarrassment, or shame, please repeat.
Still the words unclear
Impatience, anger, because it might be their fault
Why do you have to deal with the old?
'Tisn't fair, not to natures that are cold.

Margaret Topham

APOSTATES

Where are all the heroes
The role models
Archer, Clinton,
Liars.

Morally corrupt
Media-mad
Users, abusers
Of power.

How do we treat our icons
Like Diana
Haunted, hounded
To death.

Where are we all going
Without heroes
Selfish, greedy,
Alone.

Has God deserted us
Or is He there
Waiting, impotent
Hero.

Alma J Harris

LOVE OR DESIRE

My heart beats to the sound of your name,
Whether aloud or in unspoken thought.
I gasp air as I gaze at your face,
My eyes burn with a vision so sought.
Internal fires deep within my being,
Stir wildly out of control.
A desire so raw yet innocent,
Erupts from the depth of my soul.

I quake at the slightest touch,
Tremors unleash beneath my surface,
Chain reacting throughout my flesh,
Sweet convulsions increase in pace.
An aching of painful pleasure,
Courses the span of my senses.
A wildfire ungoverned by will,
Ruptures my path of defences.

I seep through the taste of your lips,
Releasing my grounded emotions.
Slick with the heat of your love,
You steal the breath from my lungs.
And as I rise through caresses of love,
Your eyes with desire do gleam.
With anticipation I tense within flames,
Then awaken from an unforgettable dream.

Mia-Joy

PANDORA'S BRAND

With the slyness of a fox,
I took you.
You were the first I ever
sinned with.
You kept me company
when I was afraid of being young.
You put me at ease,
you gave me assurance.
Maturity in a box!

Those dubious and uncertain
steps into manhood
are just distant dreams.
But I could see no reason
to give you up
until it had to be.

Now it is my blunt fingers
that feel for you,
as I scrabble with the cellophane.
I light my last, and like before,
I take that final draw.

Then I stub you out, killing
your golden fragments
one by one:
like a bird of prey
satisfying a need.
But one day, your time will come,
and *my* ashes will lie in the tray.

Anne Palmer

RESPONSE

My darling,
you ask me
to dance on
until the precipice
of life is reached.
On this summer day,
how can I answer
to a man so full of life
with such a capacity
for growth.
Your exuberant personality
such an inspiration to my
introverted quietness.
You uplift and revitalise
the mind I've got.
I need you to cancel out
my doubts, to hold my
feelings in your broad mind
and protect me from my
howls of uneasiness.
Please share my bed when
I am restless.
Fold my sharpness
in your shroud.
Drag me from the depths
of reluctance.
Sing to my senses,
continue to love me,
now,
always,
forever.

Mary Guckian

SUBMISSIONS INVITED
SOMETHING FOR EVERYONE

WOMENSWORDS 2000 - Strictly women,
have your say the female way!

POETRY NOW 2000 - Any subject,
any style, any time.

STRONGWORDS 2000 - Warning!
Age restriction, must be between 16-24,
opinionated and have strong views.
(Not for the faint-hearted)

ANCHOR BOOKS 2000 - Any subject,
light-hearted clean fun, nothing unprintable.

All poems no longer than 30 lines.
Always welcome! No fee!
Cash Prizes to be won!

Mark your envelope (eg Poetry Now) *2000*
Send to: Forward Press Ltd
Remus House, Coltsfoot Drive,
Woodston,
Peterborough, PE2 9JX

**OVER £10,000 POETRY PRIZES
TO BE WON!**
Judging will take place in October 2000